Li

MW00950817

Mrs. Coretha McCall

A King's Daughter Publishing Company LLC.

Living Sacrifice Copyright©2017
A King's Daughter Publishing Company LLC.
Newnan, Georgia
Email: AKDPublishingCo@gmail.com

Book Cover by: Rhonda McGhee
Bio Photo by: Ciherra Cooper
Published by: A King's Daughter Publishing Company LLC.
Newnan, Georgia
Distribution: Create Space

ISBN: 978-1537078878

Printed in the United States of America

Acknowledgements

To my Pastors
Steve and Lindy Hale
And Bethel Atlanta Family

Thank you for possessing the love of God and the love of family.
I have truly been changed forever.

This book is dedicated to my strong Husband and my two beautiful daughter's.
May you continue to be a living sacrifice in the earth, living as ambassadors for Jesus Christ. May you always be aware of who God really is and His beautiful Son, Jesus Christ, and what has been done on the cross. (John 10:10).
I Love you forever.

Contents

Introduction

Living Sacrifice

Romans 12:1-2

Introduction

There comes a time when we must make some decisions that will change the course of our lives forever. As a Christians once we have chosen to surrender our lives to Christ it is not the end, it is actually just the beginning. We then make a choice to begin living a life for Christ by submitting every area of our lives to him as a living sacrifice. If you are not willing to let go of the old and come into the new, what was the purpose of coming to Jesus in the first place? Too often, sons and daughters of God, heirs with Jesus Christ, live as though they have never entered into this new relationship with the Savior. It is time for us to be totally distinct in character and lifestyle. We cannot continue to operate as though we are not children of the most-high God. Without living in righteousness as a Christian our spiritual, physical, emotional, mental, and most of all, our generations are at stake. There is a standard that our father, the Almighty God has set for his children to live by and we cannot ignore it. There are many Christians who live from day to day as if they have no purpose, or calling, to assist in building the of the Kingdom of God which they have joined. It's time out for compromise and mediocrity. We must stop "playing church" it is time to go deeper, to another level, it's time to truly be a living sacrifice. There should be a visible difference in how we live because of who we are connected to. It should be so evident that we do not have to say a word. We cannot assume that we have time to make things right when it is convenient for us. Who says that you'll even get that opportunity? The enemy is doing his job, he drops the bait (deception), and then, while you're in the sin, he snatches you up so that you won't have time to repent. Don't assume that you'll have a chance to "truly repent" later. Yes, God knows your heart and, that is why we are told to be transformed by the renewing of our minds so that our heart can resemble the word which is holy. There are many things trying to get into our hearts on a daily basis trying to lead us another way but Jesus said, "I am the way, the truth, and the life." This book is a call to all sons and daughters of God to stop living below your royal heritage, and believing the lies of the enemy. In First Peter 2:9 it reads, "But ye are a chosen generation, a royal priesthood, a holy nation, a peculiar people, that ye should shew forth the praises of him who hath called you out of darkness into his marvelous light."

You don't have to go with the flow, take what you can get, stay the same, struggle in sin, or live a life of defeat in any area. You're a child of God, your father is a King over everything and he wants you to take your place and conquer everything that tries to steal, kill, or destroy you! Now is the time to surrender every area of your life for real. As you choose to obey and submit yourself to the process, watch God show you your purpose, use you to build his kingdom, fulfill the desires of your heart, and exalt you in due time.

To my Brother's and Sister's in Christ:

Many people who love the Lord are caught up in this struggle between their spirit and flesh. Apostle Paul saw and understood this he said, "For I see another law in my members, warring against the law of my mind, and bringing me into captivity to the law of sin which is in my members" (Romans 7:23). Paul recognized the issue at hand and knew something had to be done. As sons and daughters dealing with this struggle, it comes from various things, including the influence of the enemy and the world. First John 2:16 reads, "For all that is in the world, the lust of the flesh, the lust of the eyes, and the pride of life, is not of the father, but it's of the world." As a son or daughter, living in sexual sin and perversion can be deadly and destructive causing: identity issues, deception, pity, blame, embarrassment, shame, and guilt. We live in this world but we are not to be of the world. You are to impact and make change for the glory of God! Romans 12:1-2 reads, " I beseech you therefore brethren, by the mercies of God, that ye present your bodies a **living sacrifice**, holy acceptable unto God which is your reasonable service. And be not conformed to this world but be ye transformed by the renewing of your mind, that ye may prove what is that good, acceptable, and perfect will of God." You are unique, fearfully, and wonderfully made. You don't have to continue your struggle in secret and live a life in defeat. Make the decision an God will honor it, he will help you through the process. It is time to take a stand and live in holiness because the God you serve is Holy. It is time to cut some things loose, and sexual sin is one of them. There is a call to answer as a member of the body of Christ, and there is a mandate on our lives to help build the Kingdom. Let's do it without any hindrances!

Chapter 1: Between two opinions

You have been waiting and waiting to make some concrete decisions for your life. However, until you make some, you will never begin to experience the life God has planned for you. In the book of Jeremiah, verse 29:11 reads, "For I know the thoughts and the plans that I think toward you, said the Lord, thoughts of peace, and not of evil, to give you an expected end." It's crucial that we get connected with God to find out the plans he has for us, but if we don't make those choices we won't ever find out. Making decisions is something that we all have to do on a daily basis, it's a part of life. When making a decision it opens a gateway to what you've decided; good or bad. Some people believe that if they are given choices, and they choose not to accept any of them, they remain neutral, or safe. However, the reality is that even if they don't choose one of those particular choices, you have still chosen something. You've chosen to be double minded. In the book of James he talks about the characteristics of a double minded man, it is someone who is indecisive, and unstable in all of his ways (James 1:8). When you are indecisive you can't seem to make up your mind and stick to it. You are back and forth depending on how you feel or whether it is convenient. At this point you are in between two opinions. You have been halted (at a standstill) between two decisions and therefore, by default you have still chosen, which keeps you in the same place as before. This allows the enemy to come in and wreak havoc in your life. You aren't rooted and grounded in your mind about anything, this is how confusion comes in and dismantles your identity. This is also how you can begin to go backwards, miss opportunities you've been praying for, and experience unnecessary warfare from the enemy. When you wait on making decisions that you know you need to make, you end up compromising and never receiving what you were supposed. And you know what? This is just where the enemy wants; you to be out of God's will.

Sons and Daughters Hold a Standard

Sure, you can compromise on what to eat for dinner or what shoes to wear, but you can't compromise when it comes to things in life such as: your relationship with God, choosing a spouse, career, education, church, where to live, or kind of friends you will have. The areas I just mentioned are so important because they assist in shaping the course of your life and your purpose. By definition, compromising is defined settling for something else because you don't believe what you want will really happen. Did you see that? It comes from not believing! Not trusting! As children of God we must believe what God has written in his word and what he has spoken to us. When we get to a place where we don't believe, we've lost our faith. In the book of Hebrews 11:1 it reads, "Now faith is the substance of things hoped for the evidence of things not seen." No matter how we feel or what everybody else is doing we must hold on to our faith as sons and daughters of God. This is our standard, the just shall live by faith.

You can do all things through Christ who strengthens you

The greater one lives on the inside of you and given you power and authority to do all things. At this very moment you may be totally unsure but guess what? God thinks you are totally capable because you belong to him! But you know what happens sometimes… due to the fact that you can remember everything you have ever done in your whole life? You keep adding negatives to the positives! That kind of thinking makes you feel defeated and inadequate it also keeps you from making a decision to live this life fully. Jesus was sent to the world for us so that we wouldn't have to continue to be oppressed and held captive by things that make us feel invaluable. When God sent his son for you he wanted nothing but to love you. Your worth is immeasurable! You were bought with a price (the blood of Jesus) that can never be reimbursed. Can I tell you something? There's been a lie that's been going around for thousands of years. The lie is this… the enemy says, "As a Christian this is good as it gets! So you better be glad you have what you have shut up! And live with it!" This is the biggest lie ever. You do not have to live with it because God does not break his promises. As a child of God there is a covenant that is full of benefits and promises however, it is contingent on whether you believe or not and that is the decision you have to make. We live in a world and society were "seeing is believing." We live in this world and there is a great temptation to conform to the ways of it. But I plead with you do not do it! This path leads to heartache, confusion, disappointment, resentment, jealousy, envy, covetousness, and more. Proverbs 14:12 says, "There is a way that seems right unto man but the end thereof are the ways of death." This is why you cannot afford to be double minded as a Christian. Deep inside as a child of God you know there is a standard you should live by, but if you choose to compromise you will live beneath the expectation and it will impact other areas of your life.

Questions:

1. What is keeping you from making a decision?

2. Are you halted between two opinions?

3. Are you dealing with guilt or shame because of it?

4. Are you afraid you will lose something? If so what?

5. Are you ready to make some changes in your life?

Prayer:

Heavenly Father, I repent for being double minded and not believing. I ask you to give me the strength, courage and wisdom to make a decision for my life so that I may experience your goodness. In Jesus name, Amen.

Chapter 2: Renewing your mind

Renewing your mind is the one of most crucial thing's you can do in order to become a living sacrifice. The way to living a holy lifestyle as a Christian comes by reading Gods word. Everything we ever learned before our new life in Christ came through hurriedly, striving to make it happen in our own strength in our own way. But the word of God tells us in Romans 12:2, "And be not conformed to this world but be ye transformed by the renewing of your mind that ye may prove what is that good, and acceptable, and perfect will of God." As a Christian it's about trusting God, being patient with the process, and renewing our minds in order to transform. Transform means to change in form, appearance or character. When you come out of one system, the world, which consists of the lust of the eyes, the lust of the flesh, and the pride of life, it is not of the father (I John 2:16). Renewing our mind causes us to switch our thinking to the Kingdom of God's system, which is righteousness, peace and Joy in the Holy Ghost (Romans 14:17). For example have you ever went to an event and you were dressed in the wrong attire? Whether you were underdressed or overdressed you felt out of place right? This caused you to feel like you wanted to go and change your clothes so that you could fit in. Likewise, you now must change to fit into the new system, the kingdom! As a new creature in Christ this is where you are supposed to be. Too many times we are living beneath the kingdom standard. We come in the new system acting, and talking the same way until we used to until we get our minds renewed. If renewal does not take place you will be a professed Christian without any evidence (fruit) that demonstrates Christianity. Living as a Christian in righteousness is living according to the principles of the Bible which is God's word. "Likewise you now have to put on the Lord Jesus Christ, not making room for the flesh to fulfill the lust" (Rom 13:14). You have to put it on just like a pair of clothes, if you don't put on this word you will walk around naked and unprotected spiritually. Renewal of the mind keeps you clothed and protected from the attacks of the enemy. Second Corinthians 10: 3-6 says, "Though we walk in the flesh we do not war according to the flesh, for the weapons of our warfare are not carnal but are mighty through God to the pulling down of **strongholds** casting down **imaginations** and every **high thing** that exalts itself against the knowledge of God and bringing every **thought** unto the obedience of Christ and being in readiness to avenge all disobedience when your obedience is fulfilled." This is why renewing our minds is necessary for every believer. So as you can see we are flesh and live in this world but we are not subject to it, if we know what to do. A renewed mind knows how to submit to God, resist the devil and cause the enemy to flee from you. Why? Because when we "avenge all disobedience with obedience" we do the opposite of what we would usually do (as the old person) in situations and circumstances. Our mind has been renewed to live out a righteous lifestyle now. So we cast down the imaginations, thoughts that come to our mind or whatever is trying to exalt itself over God's way (the Kingdom Standard) and command it to submit to Christ.

What is a stronghold?

By definition it is a fort, or fortress- a place where a particular cause or belief is upheld. Therefore, it is in your mind and that's why it is so crucial to renew your mind. The world and our culture helped to build this stronghold or fortress of sex before or outside of marriage which is called fornication or perversion, in other words according to the Bible it is another version (perverted) of what God ordained in the sanction of marriage. If you find that you are doing things that you don't want to, trying to break free and you keep going back to sex, addictions etc.... it's because you are dealing with a stronghold. The reason you cannot stop, is because it has a hold on you. This stronghold keeps you from being a living sacrifice it is where imaginations, high things and thoughts live that is why you must cast them down and command them to come under the obedience of Christ. I going to say it again, when you do that and then submit to being obedient by doing the opposite thing suggested, that is how we avenge (punish) the enemy in that area. The mind has to be protected by the word of God, this is becoming a living sacrifice. This is why Jesus tells us in Matthew 22:17, "Love the Lord thy God with all your heart, and with all thy soul, and with all thy mind."

Imaginations, High things, and Negative Thoughts, cast it down!

According to the scripture strongholds are made up of the three things mentioned in 2 Corinthians 10:3-6. When we are exposed to these things they build a strong hold in our mind. This is how the enemy plays, he sends things into our mind as children, whether it comes through lies attacks, trauma, from people, images, or bad situations. These negative things stay in our mind and continue to try to bombard us until we act on them in a way where we believe that things will never change and build our life around them. This is why the enemy comes to kill, steal, and destroy (John 10:10) us so early in age because if he can cause any kind of dysfunction in our lives early enough he knows that it will be a challenge ahead to break free from it. It is the enemies' hopes that if he sends enough lies, and trouble into our lives we will have enough faith to believe in God or that he loves us. And when we don't believe that God loves us that affects our identity. When there is a lack of understanding on identity, there is a lack of understanding on worth. This is the strategy of the enemy to defeat us.

So I'm going to reiterate this one more time, **this is one of the most crucial areas you can begin to cultivate in your life as a Christian.** So what does renewing your mind look like? It looks like studying God's word daily, prayer, doing the word of God, guarding your eyes, ears, heart and not being influenced by the world.

When you do this you are making sure that the only things that go inside of you are building you up, making you spiritually stronger. You are fearfully and wonderfully made, a royal priesthood. Would you put trash in your refrigerator? Or rocks in your blender? Well don't put or allow anything that would hinder your relationship with God, or fragment your identity in Christ, in your life. When working on yourself to live a holy life you cannot be too passive, if you do, you will be struggling constantly. It is impossible to stay the same if you are renewing your mind with the word of God because it transforms you.

Society and its Influence

Our society has more of an influence on us than we think. It shapes are thoughts, beliefs, and what our identity will be. Our society has standards that we are expected to meet depending on: who we are, where we come from, how we look, how old we are, what kind of education and so on, you get the point. It plays a big part in how we think about sex and anything closely related to it. Perversion is everywhere you turn you will see it or hear it no matter where you go. It is constantly being promoted through commercials, sitcoms, to cartoons. It's in the airwaves working to deceive people into thinking that there is no harm or consequences and that everybody is doing it. The spirit of perversion does not discriminate, it's greedy, and its full intent is to make you lust for it at all times. Therefore, we have all kinds of things being released to us coming into our eyes, ears and hearts. The spirit of perversion is a stronghold in our society.

Questions:

1. Do you feel reading your Bible is a struggle for

you?

2. Do you feel you could read and study it more?

3. Are you struggling with living holy lifestyle as Christian?

4. Do you understand that you can cast down negative or inappropriate thoughts?

5. Do you find yourself living according to society's views instead of Christian views?

6. Do you understand that living a lifestyle contrary to the word is hindering your personal relationship with the lord and affecting the view of your identity as a son or daughter of God?

Prayer:

Lord help me to have a desire to read and study your word daily so that I may be transformed in my mind and every area of my life to live in the kingdom standard. In Jesus name, Amen.

We live in a culture and society where there is a major stronghold of perversion. This stronghold dictates that sex, pornography, masturbation, adultery and anything remotely close to it is ok. It says no matter who you are, where you are, how old or young, married or single, it's all good if you happy with it! This is a lie! This type of thinking ruins people's lives: success, friendships, marriages, and family relationships. And for those in the body of Christ it hinders our relationship with God bringing on all kinds of negative emotions with it. God does not want us to walk around feeling guilty, ashamed, embarrassed or unworthy because of something we struggle with. God wants us to be free and confident in who we are. With all of the things coming through the internet, Television, videos, radio, and through conversations, whether directly or indirectly it is no wonder why so many Christians are having a hard time living holy. The book of James says, but be ye doers of the word, and not hearers only deceiving your own selves. If you hear the word and don't do it, you're deceived. When you are deceived you believe something that is not true. Someone who is deceived usually justifies, hides or ignores their actions because they believe what they are doing is right. But guess what? There is good news the word of God can break any stronghold if you are willing to apply it to your life and do the word. The book of Hebrews says, "for the word is quick, and powerful, sharper than any two edged sword, piercing even to the dividing asunder of the soul and spirit, and of the joints and the marrow, and is a discerner of the thoughts and intents of the heart." This is how powerful the word of God is, so no matter what you are struggling with if you want to overcome it, the word of God can do it.

Chapter 3:
Protect what is sacred

Most people think that when they engage in sex the only thing being affected is the body because it's the part that is participating in the act. Now while this may be true for the moment the problem is as a Christian you have other issues you have to deal with after the "moment of pleasure" is long over. You are not just a body! Actually, you are a spirit first, if your spirit leaves your body, you'd be dead. You possess a soul, which is made up of your mind, will, and emotions. Your soul is where you think, feel, and choose. Everybody who knows you describes you according to your soulish area. You live in a body. Your body houses the first two mentioned. So as a tri-part being all three areas: spirit, soul, and body are affected when you have sex or participate in any kind of perversion. Your spirit, body and soul get the consequences of the actual act. Outside of that, even though you walk around in the body, and do what you want to do, it does not actually belong to you, it belongs to God. When Jesus died on the cross, he died for all of you. So when you accepted Jesus, by confessing with your mouth and believing with your heart that God raised him from the dead, Jesus came and took up residence in your body. So every day while you walk around doing whatever you decide to do, Jesus is with you.

That's the benefit of being a Christian, we are never alone.

Your spirit is alive and it needs to be fed the word of God in order to be sustained. In the book of Matthew 4:4, Jesus tells us, "Man shall not live by bread alone, but by every word that proceedeth out of the mouth of God." Why? Because the word of God is the spirit of God and your spirit needs his word to survive. Having access to the word strengthens our spirit, our faith, and our relationship with God. This causes us to become strong, bold, Christians full of faith, and ready to move mountains. Faith comes by hearing, and hearing by the word of God. It is the word that keeps us uplifted and encouraged, it is the food we need to sustain us at all times, through the good and bad times. The word is the bread of life we need to keep us alive on a daily basis. The spirit is alive and is the only part of us that becomes "new" when we "get saved", 2 Corinthians 5:17 says, "Therefore if any man be in Christ, he is a new creature: old things are passed away; behold all things are become new." When we confess with our mouth and believe in our hearts that God raised Jesus from the dead, then we are saved (Rom 10:9, 10). We now go from being dead to being alive in Jesus Christ. The spirit is alive to God, it wants to praise God, worship God, read, study his word, and be obedient to his leadership and commands. Matthew 26:41 tells us, "Watch and pray that ye enter not into temptation: the spirit indeed is willing but the flesh is weak. This is where the war comes in between the spirit and the soul. Paul tells us of his struggle, "I find ten a law, that, when I would do good, evil is present with me. For I delight in the law of God after the inward man: but I see another law in my members, warring against the law of my mind, and bringing me into captivity to the law of sin which is in my member.

The soul is comprised of your mind, will, and emotions. The mind has to be renewed in order to line up with our new spirit. The soul has been trained to operate independently gravitating towards what it has seen, felt, heard, and learned throughout its life. The soul steer's your life to make every decision until you have accepted Jesus as your Lord and Savior. Then it is cultivated by the word of God which is a process where the word transforms your thinking. When this happens your soul follows your new spirit and is now in control, it leads, therefore, your body has to follow. The book of Galatians 5:16 says, "This I say then, walk in the spirit, and ye shall not fulfill the lust of the flesh."

Because of all that has been kept there, it has to be weeded out, replanted, and then guarded to prevent weeds (old ways of thinking) from returning. Due to the constant bombardment of distractions that we come into contact with on a daily basis guarding it is necessary. There are all kinds of things that can trigger thoughts and have you going on a rabbit trail backwards, canceling out every bit of the word that you have learned. Taking authority over what goes into your soul is necessary. It is like soil, whatever goes in, grows and creates whatever has been planted. Images, music, words, and actions that are underlined with perversion are seeds planted. When you desire to live a life of holiness and you are struggling, and one more time, turns into one more time, you have to ask yourself "what I have planted lately?" True story, when I first began to live for Christ this was one of the first things I dealt with. Due to the fact that I came from a background where I was exposed to inappropriate images at an early age, experienced being molested, involved in a sexual relationship's as a teen and young adult, I knew deep down inside that I would need to deal with some old ways of thinking in order to live a clean lifestyle as a Christian. So little by little, I began to weed my past hurts, images, bad relationships, perverted words, music, movies, and yes my sexual relationship. It was a process and some of it was painful to deal with but it was necessary in order for me to go forward in my new life with Jesus. This was something that I knew was needed in order to get to some root issues and live a life that represented Christ. It was one of the best things I could have ever done. For the first time I felt I like I was in control of my life with Gods help. One of the fruits of the spirit is self-control, which can be found in Galatians 5:22. Due to this process and transformation I now understand my worth, and know my identity. I spent so many years believing the lie that you have to have sex to be in a relationship, to keep a man, or to get someone to be with you. I also believed the lie that everybody is doing it, and something is wrong with you if you're not doing it. It's a bunch of junk! I found out the truth, I was valuable to God and you are too! He loves you with an unconditional, everlasting love! In the Kingdom of God which you are now a part of, you do not have to settle. The kingdom is a "No Compromising Zone" because all things are possible if you believe. Believe what? That you are worth waiting for, and don't have to be tied to addictive behaviors that make you feel guilty or ashamed. God loves you! And you aren't crazy for wanting to live a holy lifestyle before God.

This is the temple of God and you are housing a Holy presence. For example, if you were carrying something very valuable in your brand new car worth millions of dollars wouldn't you be extra careful in transporting it? Yes, you would. You would make sure you were fully insured, be very particular about who rode in the car with you, and you would even figure out the clearest route to avoid a traffic jam or accident because of this precious cargo. Likewise, your body is precious and is carrying a holy presence. God is concerned about your body because that is where his Son lives. God went through a whole lot (sent his son to die for you) to make sure that you could have access to him all the time and spend eternity with him. You should not just treat it like anything, the same precaution you would take to transport that very valuable item is no different to how you would preserve your body. This really has to do with how you view yourself. Do you know who you really are? Are you sure you understand your true identity as a child of God? God has expectations for you, "For this is the will of God, even your sanctification that you should abstain from fornication (I Thess 4:3). "But fornication and all uncleanness, or covetousness, let it not be once named among you, as becometh saints" (Ephesians 5:3). Why? Because you are royalty and you do not have to succumb to the ways of the world. God's way is better. God wants nothing but the best for you, God knows and understands your worth. When you participate in sexual sin as a Christian, you sin against your own body causing death to come upon it through, sickness, disease, emotional distress, mental distress, spiritual distress and death. So in the end, you are worse off than you were before. The book of 2 Peter 2:20 reads, "For if after they have escaped the pollutions of the world through the knowledge of the Lord and Savior Jesus Christ, they are entangled therein, and overcome, and the latter end is worse with them than the beginning." In the book of I Corinthians 6:18 says, "Flee fornication. Every sin that a man doeth is without the body; but he that committeth fornication sinneth against his own body". There is a cost for sin, it is spiritual death and we know with the statistics sometimes premature physical death (Rom 6:23). Neither one of them are worth it. Staying entangled in the bondage of sexual sin and perversions, will have you trying to get out of a web that will cost you everything: your relationship with God, your identity, your purpose, blessings, vision, dreams, plans and much more. When you surrendered your life to Christ you were set free by a king. Why continue in something that will only keep you captive? Receive all that Christ has done for you in every area today. He did it on the cross and it is finished.

Questions:

1. Can you identify where you are right now in your life?

2. Do you understand that it is a choice of love to stop certain behaviors?

3. Can you see yourself living a clean life?

4. Does sound like something you can do at this time?

5. Do you understand everything that is involved as a son or daughter?

Prayer:

Jesus I ask you to forgive me for my sins that I have committed against my body. I ask you to give me wisdom, strength and courage to apply these new lifestyle changes to my life. In Jesus name, Amen.

Chapter 4:
Trying to Fill a Space Meant for God

I wasted many years in my life trying to fill a void that I just could not explain, I tried looking for love in all the wrong places. I was trying to get to a place where I felt valued, worthy, significant, accepted, and loved. Well since then I have come to a conclusion… this place that feels empty… was meant for the Love of God only and can never be filled with anything else. At the end of the day people want to be loved for who they are flaws, mistakes and all. The problem with this is that we try to use things and imperfect people to fill this God sized void. I found out that no person, pet, amount of money, thing, or addiction can fill it, it will only temporary. Our father, God, created us with the space for him because he created us to be with him. However, in the search for true love and acceptance we get bruised, battered, cheated, and mistreated trying to fill this space that only God can fill. We get caught up in other things that give us a false sense of identity, a "feeling" of being loved which results in disappointment in the end. Because the disappointment hurts so bad everything else becomes minimized.

Using Sex as your Capital

Capital is something you use to make sure you get what you want. Many sons and daughters of God use sex as their capital to feel loved, feel accepted, have companionship or feel validated. While this is something that hinders every part of a Born- again believer's life as well as their personal relationship with God what many do not know is that it is an idol. It is an idol because there is a sacrifice made to get what they want. Unfortunately, after the sacrifice to have sex in order to "feel something" is made the thing desired never comes into fruition. Because created sex to be between to people, a man and a woman in a covenant relationship. This trade-off is nothing more than a quick fix, very temporary, it covers or soothes the area briefly but it never heals or fills that space. Using your body that does not belong to you, for the purpose to get what you want and deciding to relinquish the purpose, plan, process and promise of your life for a moment of pleasure is selfish. As a child of God once you surrender your life to Christ you belong to God I Corinthians 6:19 reads, "What? Know ye not that your body is the temple of the Holy Ghost which is in you, which ye have of God, and ye are not your own?

The Consequence of Sexual Sin as a Child of God

As soon as it stops "making you feel" loved, accepted, or validated, you will feel emptier than before. Realize that all though you are having fun for the moment you will not get the true love you're looking for. So guess what happens? Then you're addicted to the sexual relationship, perversion "and you just can't stop" because it makes you at least feel something. It entangles you to the spirit of perversion which gives you a false sense of worth and dependency, keeping you in bondage to the act. As a son or daughter of God the word encourages us in the book of Galatians 5:1, "Stand fast therefore in the liberty wherewith Christ hath made us free, and be not entangled again with the yoke of bondage."

Now, I do understand that there are people who are not seeking (or so blinded by the enemy) to stop what they are doing. However, even with that there is still a root cause for the behavior, something has happened, and something is missing. The void needs to be filled with God's love and those who don't want out of the cycle will continue to try to fill it for the rest of their lives while being numb to it. The love of Jesus is so powerful that whatever you are presently struggling with if you surrender it and seek his help, you will be filled with the love you have always been wanting. Don't continue to go in and out of relationships feeling numb, participating in things that make you feel burdened, guilty, ashamed and condemned. Come to the light.

Questions:

1. Are you getting some clarity about how important you are as a son or daughter?

2. Are you tired of the same old thing and doing the same old thing?

3. Do you know what the void is?

4. Do you understand that this space is only for God?

5. Are you ready to fill that void with God?

Prayer:

Jesus, I need you to help me. I am ready to change my life. I don't want to continue to try to fill this void with anything else but you. I submit to the process.

Chapter 5:
Deliverance from Intrusions and Violations

The enemy comes to kill, steal and destroy. Anything bad that has ever happened in your life was a plan of the enemy. He has a goal to stop and hinder you no matter what. There are too many Christians fighting to get their freedom, trying to regain what the enemy has stolen from them. Unfortunately though, after some have entered into the body of Christ and have been given freedom, some still end up bound by the lies of the enemy concerning their past and it continues to dictate the course of their lives as a Christian. Listen, everything that was taken by the enemy, God has a replacement called newness. Isiah 43: 18, 19 reads, "Remember not the former things neither consider the thigs of old, Behold I will do new thing, now it shall spring forth shall you not know it? I will even make ways in the wilderness and rivers in the desert." God wants to replace anything in your life that was taken or was not from him. God wants to restore you, making you whole and complete.

Intrusions

Many people are carrying loads and loads of baggage that we cannot see. These bags weigh us down, dictating how we operate and how we view everything in life such as: relationships, success, and our worth. Getting healed and delivered is crucial in order to be able to function effectively as a Christian person. It is also important in order to walk in peace in our hearts and minds. Healing brings newness, and restoration to our lives, like a broken and bruised knee that has been healed. Being delivered means we're free from bondage, and God gives us the ability to maintain the freedom we have been given through things like the word of God and prayer.

There are two areas I would like to identify that hold people captive, Intrusions and violations. These two mentioned are from the enemy and carry lies, causing people to live lives that are dictated by fear, shame, guilt, anger, bitterness, confusion, hurt and pain. By definition an Intrusion is the act of someone invading your life, without permission.

The enemy intrudes into our lives with the intentions of killing, stealing, and destroying us so that we are not able to live for Christ effectively. The enemy comes into our lives in times were we are vulnerable. Many people have experienced intrusions as children as well as at adult age. Children are innocent and helpless and unfortunately, they can be taken advantage of and their lives can be changed forever due to an attack of the enemy. Personally, I experienced an intrusion as a child, my baby sitter thought it was o.k. to allow me to watch inappropriate movies, this disturbed my innocent mind and perverted by childhood thinking. I didn't want to watch the movies but the enemy was trying to ruin my life. This intrusion opened up the door for me to be molested. This forever changed my life because from that time forward, my thoughts were perverted which led me to have sex early in age as a teenager. Although this would seem to be the norm, acceptable in society being a sexually active teenager. The seed that was planted was meant to destroy my life. Due to that intrusion in my life as a little girl, it grew until it produced the fruit of fornication. I continued on this road up until the age twenty-five and let me tell you something in all those years of being sexually active nothing good came from it. Every relationship ended in with some kind of: hurt, shame, rejection, embarrassment, or disappointment. Eventually I surrendered my spirit, soul, and body to Jesus Christ at twenty-five years old while I was eight months pregnant with my first child. Deep in my heart I knew there had to be a better way, so I started my journey to healing.

Violations

This is another experience that constantly has people feeling insignificant and trying to fill a void with sex, drugs, or some other kind of perversion. It is called a violation and by definition it is when someone has interfered against your personal rights. Being violated is serious, and it's not your fault. This act of being violated promotes fear and lies about who you really are. As I mentioned earlier about being molested, that was a violation and it was meant to destroy me. Anytime the enemy uses people to hurt you it is meant to kill, steal or destroy your life (John 10;10). Violations can hold you captive in your soul (which is your mind, will, and emotions) and control your behavior. This is why healing and deliverance are so key. Intrusions and Violations keep you feeling trapped and fearful. They also produce hopelessness, making you think there is no use in trying to change your life since those things have already happened. This is a lie and a trick of the enemy. Intrusions and violations produce fear of all kinds and rejection.

Fear and Rejection

Fear and rejection are also from the enemy, it is something that has been used to keep the people of God at a standstill for many years. These two things also keep people from experiencing God's perfect plan for their lives. The spirit of fear is a holding cell, it imprisons the person who is fearful. Let me tell you something, as a child of God fear does not belong to you. Second Timothy 1:7, lets us know, "For God has not given us a spirit of fear but of power and of love and of a sound mind." You possess power, love and a sound mind! This Power is called "Dunamis" which means miracle working power that comes from God, love is Agape love the love of Christ that conquers everything, and sound mind is to be disciplined, and have the ability to make good judgement. There is equipment inside of you to stay free of fear! God has given us all three of these things we can overcome the enemy and his tactics by using what we have. It will take some intentional thought and will be a process to do this, however, it can be done. We do not have to live in fear. So I want to encourage you to begin to deal with whatever fears you have so that you can live a life of total freedom.

Rejection is something the enemy tries to make sure we experience as early as possible because he knows that if that happens when God comes to extend his love the person who experienced the rejection will not know how to receive it because of the hurt and pain of being rejected. There are many fruits of rejection, meaning people can have various behaviors or attitudes from being rejected. For example, the person who has been rejected may not trust people or their motives for wanting to be connected to them. Or they may be people pleasers and do whatever it takes to get people to like them. Additionally, they may have low self-esteem and struggle with their identity. God has also given us a way to get free from rejection too! Just getting a true understanding of how much God loves you is a way to get free from rejection and you can find that information in his word and through prayer also. Outside of those ways mentioned another way to get free is forgiveness.

Forgiveness Frees You

Yes, Forgiveness. Forgiving someone for what they did to you is not for them, **IT IS FOR YOU**. When I talk to people about this I noticed that people really feel like that if they forgive, they are letting the other person get away with what they did wrong. First off they do not get away with hurting anyone. Because God is a just God and he will judge what has been wrongfully done to you. Listen, when you forgive, it's setting you free! When you choose not to forgive you hold them captive, but it locks you up too! Think about it, if when you think about or see that person who offended or hurt you, do you change? If the answer is yes, everything about you changes, your emotions, and behavior switch, you are not free. Anyone who can do that has control of you, and your freedom is non-existent. This can be detrimental to your relationship with Christ, affecting your physical health, your mental and spiritual health. Unforgiveness can cause death in all these areas. Forgiveness brings life. Jesus brought life to us by forgiving us for our sins. In doing that we are now sons and daughters of God and get to live eternally with Him. We reap the benefits of the entire salvation package because God has forgiven us. The salvation package includes freedom. When you choose not to forgive you aren't getting the whole package. Make a choice and forgive. You will find that you sleep better, act differently, and have a joy that was not there before. I'm not going to say that it's easy and that it doesn't hurt to go through the healing process but it is necessary and for your benefit. You can forgive because the greatest forgiver lives on the inside of you and greater is he that lives on the inside of you than he who is in the world (1 John 4:4).

Questions:

1. Are you able to identify an intrusion in your life?

2. Are you ready to give it over to God and allow him to take care of it?

3. Are you able to identify a violation in your life?

4. Are you ready to give that over to God?

5. Is fear and rejection evident in your life?

6. Do you want to be free?

7. Is forgiveness something that is hard for you to do?

8. Do you understand that you will need to make a

decision to forgive just like Jesus forgave you?

9. Do you understand that it will be something that you will need to do soon?

Prayer:

Lord, I ask you to heal my heart and mind from all of the hurt and pain due to the intrusions and violations that I have experienced. I ask you to help me in this area, I also want to be free from fear and rejection. You said, "Many are the afflictions of the righteous but you would deliver me out of them all." I believe you will. Please help me through this process. Amen.

Chapter 6:
Anybody Just Won't Do

Listen, as lonely as it may get sometimes, not just anybody will do it for you. When you chose to settle for someone because you don't want to be by yourself, you are messing with your destiny. Every person that you connect to is not necessarily supposed to be in your life. God will send people in your life to help you get where you need to be however, the enemy will send people to destroy your life also. There are time when there is an assignment from the enemy to stop you and he will use people. If you are lonely, struggling with your identity, and tired of waiting for the right person. This type of person, the exact profile I just described, is a prime candidate for the enemy to come after. This is why you can't afford not to understand your worth or know your true identity. God's thoughts and plans for you are good and not evil to give you an expected end (Jerimiah 29:11).

Know Who and Why You Are Connected to Them

The Bible has many great examples to help us get an understanding of what we should and should not do in our lives. For an example, there is a great man, who was called by God, his name, Sampson, God used him very mightily to judge and deliver Israel for twenty years. The only problem was Sampson seemed to always find himself connected to the wrong people. Sampson loved women, and not only did he love women but he loved women who were not going to have his best interest at all. In Judges, Chapter 13 through 16, you will find that he is a man of God on an assignment. God sends him to spy out the enemy, to get strategy on how to defeat them but he gets distracted by what he sees. Each time he is distracted there is a woman he wants to have. These women had a seducing and enticing spirit operating in them that helped them to cause trouble and his eventual demise. The first wife betrays him by asking him for an answer to a riddle and then gives the answer to his enemy in order to receive goods. After that big ordeal she ends up marrying his best man from his wedding. The second wife, Delilah, manipulates him into telling her what makes him so strong, causing him to lose his strength by telling his enemies that his supernatural strength comes from his hair. Due to

Sampson's lack of wisdom in knowing why and who he was supposed to be connected to, Delilah his wife, who is the enemy, is the cause of his death. We must be careful about who we connect to in this season. Everybody that comes into our lives is not for us to connect to on a personal relationship level. Sampson saw beautiful women that he wanted, but he lacked the wisdom and discernment on who they really were in the spirit. Connecting to the wrong people can alter your life and take you down a path that was not intended by God. I want to encourage you to love the Lord with all your heart, mind, soul, and strength. Surrender your whole life to God and understand what season you are in when it comes to people. Be a person of prayer and ask God for wisdom or discernment concerning the people you connect ourself to. In addition, I want to encourage you to ask other people to pray for you. Doing these things will help you to stay connected to the right people and possess good judgement on relationships and the purpose of them.

Questions:

1. Do you know your worth and how important it is to know who and why you are connected to people?

2. Have you identified why you are in the relationship with these people?

3. Can you discern seducing and enticing spirits?

4. Are you willing to pray about those you are connected to and allow God to give you or show you the answer?

5. Are you trusting God about your relationships?

6. Do you need wisdom and discernment on this subject? Ask God to give it to you.

Prayer:

Father, I come before you asking you to give me the courage and the wisdom and discernment to identify the purpose of my relationships with people. I want to live for you and trust you with my whole life.

Chapter 7:
Godly Lifestyle

It is something about serving God that is so advantageous. Although we may not come into the relationship with Christ with the idea of what do I get out of it? It is not hard to see from the scriptures that God wants us to live a good life filled joy and peace. In Psalms 16:11 it says, " Thou will show me the path of life, in thy presence is fullness of joy at thy right hand there are pleasures forever ore." He provides us with various ways to experience his goodness and to live a life feeling encouraged, victorious and successful. As children of God we are expected to live by a certain standard and there some ways to maintain that standard. Prayer, meditation of God's word, declaration, and praise are just some of the tools we can use to keep us grounded in the principles of God, holding to the standards, enabling us have good success in order to be a living sacrifice in this world (Joshua 1:8).

The Power of Prayer

Prayer is so powerful! As underestimated as it is, the effectiveness cannot be denied, without it nothing good would happen on the earth. It is the prayers of the righteous that help to establish the good on earth as it is in heaven. You must pray as a Christian. It should be a part of your everyday life. Prayer is petitioning (asking) God for whatever it is you want to see happen. It strengthens you as a person and brings you closer to God. You get to know God and God tells you who you are and all of his great thoughts and plans for you. It is in this time of conversation with God that you get an understanding about how much you are loved and learn your true identity. Whatever you want to see happen in your life that lines up with the word of God, pray that. Pray the word of God over yourself. God's promises are yes and amen for your life. If you don't pray for yourself who will? Keep doing this consistently until you see what you have been praying for. Don't get tired of praying, it will come to pass if you have patience and believe. In the book of Galatians, Paul encourages us not to get weary in doing well because if we don't faint we will reap whatever we've believed for (Galatians 6:9). God will come through but patience is required.

Meditation

Taking Gods word and intentionally rolling it over in your mind again and again, is meditation. This is setting a foundation that cannot be shaken or moved. God encouraged Joshua to meditate and said the end result of doing this was success! Who doesn't want success? My idea of success may be different from yours, but regardless of what your interpretation maybe be, it is still success to the individual. You can apply this to your life if you want to be a living sacrifice. For example, one of the things that I began to do to remain celibate while I as single, was to take scriptures pertaining to living a clean life.

I had scriptures posted on my mirrors, walls, and refrigerator. Meditating on God's word helped me to stay focused and accomplish my goal of remaining celibate until marriage.

Declaration

When you open your mouth you create an atmosphere. Proverbs reads, "Life and death is in the power of the tongue and they that love it shall eat the fruit thereof. In simpler terms, you will have whatever you say. Therefore, watch your words because you have power and authority! This can be one of biggest challenges, saying only what God's word says concerning your situation instead of what you see. As a son or daughter we are not to speak anything but life. When you declare Gods word you are planting seeds, bringing life. You are prophecy! Speaking things that you don't presently see into existence. That is what our father did! He spoke and it was. Declaration build's your faith and creates an atmosphere of confidence, and expectation in God to do just what you said. If you are not sure on what to declare find scriptures in the Bible that you want to possess in your life and speak them over your life in full expectation that it will happen.

Praise is necessary!

Give Glory to God! When you sing praise and have a thankful heart towards God it breaks whatever is holding you captive. This is one of the main tools that I use. I love to praise God. I sing and sing in my house for hours because I love to worship the Lord and when I'm done I feel so much better. It's like the weight of the world has been taken off my shoulders. I have so much peace and joy, I feel like I can conquer anything! Praise is necessary. It paralyzes the enemy, so lift up praises to God! There is nothing the enemy can do to stop you when you are full of praise and thankfulness. The enemy may come but that will be it! The trouble may come to stop you but it will not prosper! God will prevail! So praise God for who he is in your life and what has already been done.

Questions:

1. Do you think you have a good prayer life? If not why?

2. Do you meditate on God's word? If not why?

3. Do you declare Gods word over your life? If not why?

4. Are you a person of Praise? If not why?

5. Are you willing to do these things to grow closer to God? If so how often?

Prayer:

Lord I ask you to help me become a person that has a lifestyle devoted to you through prayer, meditation, declaration and praise. Create in me a clean heart and renew a right spirit within me.

Chapter 8:
Have Faith in God

As sons and daughter's we are to be people of faith. Now faith is the substance of things hoped for the evidence of things not seen (Hebrews 11:1). Although you cannot see it, it's there. Faith without works is dead. The works is the obedience to follow through in what the word say's for you to do and what you say you believe. If you have faith that you are able to live a clean lifestyle. Then with the faith you will need to create safeguards for yourself in order to achieve the goal, this is the works. You are setting yourself up to receive what you believe. Walk by faith and not by sight (2 Corinthians 4:7). Anyone that has decided to come into the body of Christ God has been given a measure of faith. Romans 12:3 reads, " For I say through the grace given unto me, to every man that is among you, not to think of himself more highly than he ought to think: but to think soberly according as God hath dealt to every man the measure of faith."

So according to the scripture you have a measure of have faith. Your faith in God can keep you from sexual sin. However, this is totally contingent upon you. The word tells us to think soberly which is to have a sound mind, to exercise self-control. If you are at a place where you are participating in things that you really don't want to do, then you lack self-control or the ability to think soberly of yourself. Listen, God wants to help you but you have to be willing to cooperate with the help. There is no reason to be in bondage to addictive behaviors, Christ has finished it on the cross, and he has overcome everything! You just need to follow the instruction manual (the Bible). When you gave your life to Jesus Christ the understanding should be "when I do this, my life will be better." That means everything that was in your past, should now be over. Why stay or go back to it? While one reason could be, that you're just not ready to give it up because you like it or you're afraid of the outcome. Another reason someone would stay, or go back to something that was not good mentally, physically or spiritually could be that they lacked understanding about who they really are as a son or daughter. When you don't know your full identity and purpose, things can look and feel impossible. But the word of God say's all things are possible to him that believe. You may not see how you can live this sacrificial lifestyle with all of the pressures of pleasure around you, but can I tell you a secret? It's in what you cannot see that is the most important. Have faith in God that you can do this. Living a Holy life will reap its covenant promises. Christians are struggling, and they don't feel like waiting until marriage because it doesn't seem realistic and reachable to them. The word tells us to walk in the spirit and we will not fulfill the lust of the flesh Galatians 5:16). Honestly, this may be the problem, spiritual people who need God to be involved in a spiritual battle, trying to operate in a carnal (flesh) mindset in dealing with this particular issue. So make a decision and ask God to help you with the "How". God will honor you and begin to give you strength, courage, and wisdom in this area.

Questions:

1. Have you ever asked God to help you in this area?

2. Do you have faith to believe that you can live a clean lifestyle?

3. Do you have a desire to live a holy lifestyle?

4. Is there anything blocking your thinking preventing you from moving forward in this?

5. Are you ready to apply the works to your faith in order to get this accomplished?

Chapter 9:
Your True Identity

Your true identity comes from God. It does not come from your past mistakes, rejection or what people have said about you. Although all of that stuff seems very hard to dismiss the truth is… they are lies from the enemy to keep us stuck. God actually has a great plan and knows you by name. Don't believe the hype of the enemy! You are fearfully and wonderfully made in the sight of God. God created you to succeed, to experience life and have it more abundantly (John 10; 10).

Unfortunately, the identity of a child of God will always be under attack. Jesus' identity was attacked by the enemy in the wilderness so we should not expect anything different. We live in a world where conformity is normal and anyone who decides to live for Jesus Christ for real will experience some form of an attack (2 Timothy 3:12). Unfortunately, we have been so overwhelmed by this,that we have begun to get weary in doing good, and have surrendered to conformity. If we bite at the lures set for us, changing everything about us, talking negatively about ourselves because we are different, people will never be introduced or impacted by the true identity of the believer. Let me tell you something, in order for you to be content in who you are, you will have to get the truth from your father, the almighty God. God created you and predestined you to be on this earth. The lie that continues to annoy and irritate the child of God is…"you are not who you think and say you are because…" This has been a tactic of the enemy since the beginning of time. The enemy did the same thing to Jesus while he was on his forty day fast (Matt 4:4). However, Jesus had an answer for the enemy every time! The word came straight from the word of God (Matthew 4: 1-11). After three attempts the enemy finally left him alone. The truth about who you really are is in the word of God, it comes from **The Almighty God** himself. You will need to read, study, and hear the word in order to begin to walk in your true identity by faith. Once you embrace the truth of what God really thinks about you, you will begin to walk in a confidence that will be unshakeable and uncompromising. You will begin to realize that you were living below royal standards as a son or daughter of God. The standards of righteousness are in the book that has been left for us to live by. They come with a safety net and plenty of blessings. And there is one more lie I want to expose, what you **do not** know can hurt you! (Hosea 4:6). True story, I remember when I first "got saved" and began to read my bible. I intentionally read promises, and encouraging words of assurance that God loved me and would never leave me because of the rejection I experienced. I had a challenging time believing it deep down inside. Because I had been rejected so many times before in my life that I had to read, meditate, and hear the word in order for it to become a part of me, there was some reconstruction that had to take place in my soul, it had to go really deep. Now even in my most difficult times because I have experienced his word, I now believe and can count on God to be there for me no matter what. When you don't realize who you are you will behave out of character and accept things that you don't have to. God says you are good, a conqueror, holy, a royal priesthood, a chosen generation, beautiful, blessed, righteous, loved, free, healed, delivered, the head, above, wealthy, a new creation, a friend, justified, redeemed, accepted , called, a fellow-heir with Christ, forgiven, predestined, sealed, fearfully and wonderfully made, seated in heavenly places, a workmanship created to produce good works, bought with a price, priceless, light, a citizen of heaven, his child and the list goes on! A living sacrifice is what you are called to be, set aside for his use to do great things in the earth. You will do all that God has created you to do! God does not start a work that cannot be completed! Will you submit to the process? "For you are God's handiwork created in Christ Jesus, to do good works so you can do all that he has planned for you (Ephesians 2:10). May God Bless you as you run this race that is set before you, be strong and courageous finishing strong (Eccles 9:11, Hebrews 12:1, Joshua 1:8).

About The Author

Coretha McCall is the Founder of Esther Project Ministries, located in Georgia. Esther Project Ministries, goal is to get women equipped in every area of their lives for the building up of the kingdom of God. Coretha is a teacher she is called to perfect the saints, for the work of the ministry, for the edifying of the body of Christ, speaking the truth in love that we may grow up in Jesus who is the head of all things (Ephesians 4:12,15). She teaches in small groups, women's ministries, conferences, seminars. She also does workshops providing strategies and tools to build better lives. In addition she disciple's women by walking along side and encouraging them to live righteous lives no matter what the moral climate shifts too. She's an author, worshiper, songwriter, and leader for Christ. She loves to empower people to move forward in their dreams and live out the life God has purposed for them. She resides in Georgia with her husband and two children.

Now available!
Order your Book Today on Amazon or
Create space E-store!

Now Available on iTunes, and Amazon!
Order your copy today!

Contact Information and Booking:
Email: estherprojectministries@gmail.com
Website: www.corethamccall.com
Facebook: Coretha McCall or Esther Project
Ministries LLC.
 770-376-5554